Bible Story
COLOR BY DOTS

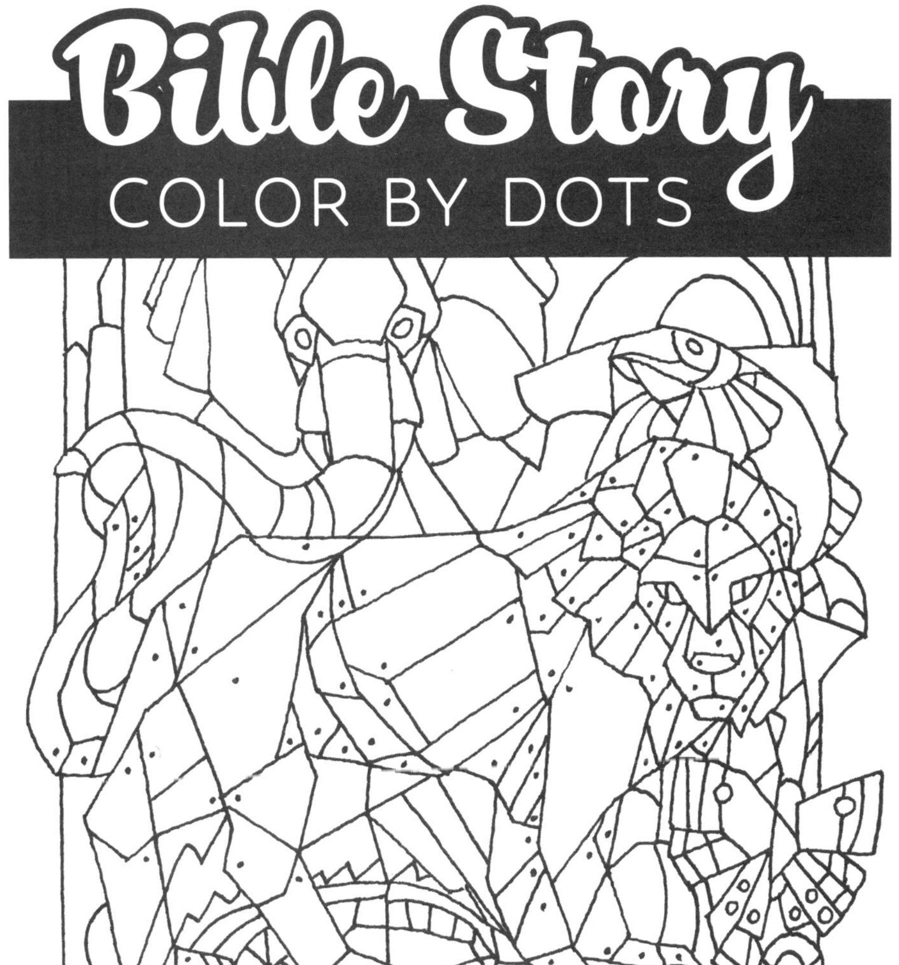

Illustrated by Michael Denman

305800232025

God told Adam and Eve they could eat from every tree
except one. Then something tempted Eve,
and she disobeyed God. So did Adam.

Color in the spaces with dots to see the picture.

After the rain stopped, Noah sent something out of the ark to see if the land was dry again.

Color in the spaces with dots to see the picture.

Joseph wondered if his brothers were still mean. To test them, he had something hidden in his brother Benjamin's sack.

Color the spaces with dots to see the picture.

God's people were wandering in the desert for a long time. God gave them manna to eat, but they complained and wanted something else.

Color the spaces with dots to see the picture.

The king wanted David to wear his heavy armor to fight Goliath. David chose a different way to fight the giant.

Color the spaces with dots to see the picture.

Jonah got on a boat to run away from God. A huge storm came,
and he told the sailors to throw him overboard.
God sent something to swallow Jonah.

Color the spaces with dots to see the picture.

The king made a law that people could only pray to him. Daniel would only pray to God. When Daniel was thrown into a den of hungry animals, God kept Daniel safe.

Color the spaces with dots to see the picture.

A king chose beautiful Esther to be his new queen.
Later, she saved God's people.

Color the spaces with dots to see the picture.

Nehemiah was the king's cupbearer.
He made sure the king's wine was safe for him to drink.

Color the spaces with dots to see the picture.

At different times, Mary and Joseph each saw someone who told them Mary would give birth to God's Son.

Color the spaces with dots to see the picture.

When Mary and Joseph were in Bethlehem,
someone special came into their lives—Jesus!

Color the spaces with dots to see the picture.

Jesus told a story about a young man who left home, wasted all his money, and had to get a job feeding animals. Even then, his father still loved him.

Color the spaces with dots to see the picture.

A woman knelt by Jesus, crying because she was so sorry for her sins. She poured costly perfume on Jesus' feet. Jesus told her, "Your sins are forgiven."

Color the spaces with dots to see the picture.

Many times, Jesus would go away by Himself to talk to God.
He taught His disciples how to pray too.

Color the spaces with dots to see the picture.

Jesus loves us so much that He gave His life for us. If we believe in Jesus, we will be saved from our sins and live with Him in heaven someday.

Color the spaces with dots to see the picture.